PowerKiDS
Readers
SEA FRIENDS

DOLPHINS

SAM DRUMLIN

PowerKiDS
press™

New York

Published in 2013 by The Rosen Publishing Group, Inc.
29 East 21st Street, New York, NY 10010

First Edition

Editor: Amelie von Zumbusch
Book Design: Liz Gloor and Colleen Bialecki

Photo Credits: Cover Juergen & Christine Sohns/Picture Press/Getty Images; p. 5 Masa Ushioda/age fotostock/Getty Images; pp. 7, 19, 21 iStockphoto/Thinkstock; p. 9 Tubuceo/Shutterstock.com; Panoramic Images/Getty Images; p. 13 Christian Musat/Shutterstock.com; p. 15 Stockbyte/Thinkstock; p. 17 Stephen Frink/Stone/Getty Images; p. 21 iStockphoto/Thinkstock; p. 23 Anna Segeren/Shutterstock.com.

Library of Congress Cataloging-in-Publication Data

Drumlin, Sam.
  Dolphins / by Sam Drumlin. — 1st ed.
      p. cm. — (Powerkids readers: sea friends)
  Includes index.
  ISBN 978-1-4488-9641-7 (library binding) — ISBN 978-1-4488-9740-7 (pbk.) —
  ISBN 978-1-4488-9741-4 (6-pack)
  1. Dolphins—Juvenile literature. I. Title.
  QL737.C432D78 2013
  599.53—dc23
                                    2012020315

Manufactured in the United States of America

CPSIA Compliance Information: Batch #W13PK3: For Further Information contact Rosen Publishing, New York, New York at 1-800-237-9932

CONTENTS

Dolphins like to play!

They are smart.

They live in the sea.

They can dive deep.

They breathe air.

They breathe through **blowholes**.

Fish are their main food.

A group of dolphins is
a **pod**.

A baby is a **calf**.

Mothers most often have one calf at a time.

WORDS TO KNOW

blowhole

calf

pod

INDEX

WEBSITES

Due to the changing nature of Internet links, PowerKids Press has developed an online list of websites related to the subject of this book. This site is updated regularly. Please use this link to access the list:
www.powerkidslinks.com/pkrsf/dolph/